How a
Plane
Is Made

By Amy Hayes

Gareth Stevens
PUBLISHING

Please visit our website, www.garethstevens.com. For a free color catalog of all our high-quality books, call toll free 1-800-542-2595 or fax 1-877-542-2596.

Cataloging-in-Publication Data

Hayes, Amy.
How a plane is made / by Amy Hayes.
p. cm. — (Engineering our world)
Includes index.
ISBN 978-1-4824-3931-1 (pbk.)
ISBN 978-1-4824-3932-8 (6-pack)
ISBN 978-1-4824-3933-5 (library binding)
1. Airplanes — Juvenile literature. 2. Airplanes — Parts — Juvenile literature. I. Hayes, Amy. II. Title.
TL547.H35 2016
629.134—d23

First Edition

Published in 2016 by
Gareth Stevens Publishing
111 East 14th Street, Suite 349
New York, NY 10003

Copyright © 2016 Gareth Stevens Publishing

Designer: Samantha DeMartin
Editor: Ryan Nagelhout

Photo credits: Cover, p. 1 MO_SES Premium/Shutterstock.com; background Jason Winter/Shutterstock.com; caption boxes stoonn/Shutterstock.com; p. 5 Andrey Armyagov/Shutterstock.com; p. 7 honglouwawa/Shutterstock.com; p. 9 Pressmaster/Shutterstock.com; p. 11 Joe McNally/Getty Images News/Getty Images; p. 13 PASCAL PAVANI/AFP/Getty Images; p. 15 Frank Wasserfuehrer/Shutterstock.com; p. 17 (main) Konstantin Yolshin/Shutterstock.com; p. 17 (inset) StudioSmart/Shutterstock.com; p. 19 Bloomberg/Bloomberg/Getty Images; p. 20 GoneWithTheWind/Shutterstock.com.

Printed in the United States of America

CPSIA compliance information: Batch #CS16GS: For further information contact Gareth Stevens, New York, New York at 1-800-542-2595.

Contents

Words in the glossary appear in **bold** type the first time they are used in the text.

Amazing Airplanes

Airplanes fly thousands of feet up in the air. They're one of the fastest and safest ways to travel all over the world. Small planes fit just a few people, but bigger ones seat hundreds. A trip on an airplane is called a flight.

Airplanes are amazing, huge machines that fly all over the world. But how do they get up in the air? How are they made? What makes an airplane work?

Building Blocks

There are about 200,000 airplane flights each day from all corners of the world.

Airplanes help people fly just about everywhere!

5

The Science of Flight

Airplanes use a force called lift to get them up in the air. Lift is created by the shape of the airplane's wings. To create lift, the plane has to be moving very fast. When a plane moves forward, wind whips over and under the wings.

Because of the wings' shape, the wind flowing under them moves much faster than the wind flowing over them. This creates lift and pushes the plane up into the air.

Building Blocks

Lift is the force that moves a plane upward, while the force moving the plane forward is called thrust. Airplane **engineers** learned how to use these forces to get planes in the sky.

Physics is the science that teaches us how forces such as lift make objects move.

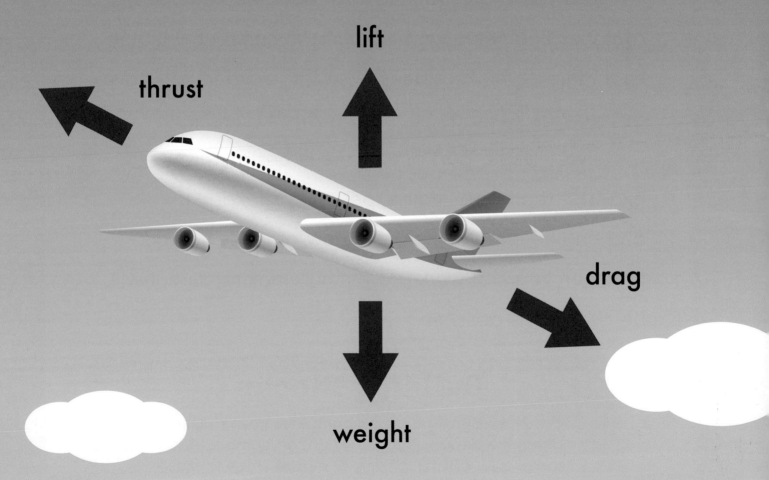

lift

thrust

drag

weight

Designing a Plane

Did you know that it takes many people to **design** a plane? Engineers work together to come up with the best ideas to make planes fly. A large plane can have as many as 4,000 engineers working to design it!

Every single part of a plane is designed by **experts**. There are chair experts, wing experts, and engine experts. Before a new plane is first put together, years of work are put into making sure it will be as safe as possible.

Building Blocks

When designing a plane, engineers have to think about the airports the planes will be going to. They spend a lot of time looking at airport maps to make sure their planes are the right size for airport **runways** and can fly long enough to reach certain airports.

Engineers carefully map out exactly where all the parts of a plane will go. These plans are called blueprints.

Time to Test

Engineers use math to create the best designs they can. Once a part of an airplane is designed, it's time to test it! Each part of a plane has to be individually tested. This means each part is tested on its own to make sure it can handle all sorts of **situations**.

If a part fails a test, it has to be redesigned. Engineers use computer **simulations** and wind-tunnel models. Engineers even make tiny engines to scale just to make sure everything works properly.

Building Blocks

Wind tunnels are used to test models of the plane to make sure it can fly! Cars and other **vehicles** use wind tunnels to make sure air moves over their bodies properly.

It takes many hours of testing before a full-size plane is ready to be built.

Getting the Parts

Small airplanes can be manufactured, or made, all in one place. These smaller airplanes seat only one or two people. However, big airplanes have millions of parts! Some of the parts are made at other locations and shipped to where the plane is being built.

Once all the parts from other places are brought in, it's time to bring them to the hangar, which is the big building where the plane is put together.

Building Blocks

The hangar in Everett, Washington, where Boeing's 747 plane is manufactured is so tall that clouds used to collect inside it! Boeing had to add a system to better move the air around inside to stop them from forming.

One of Airbus's biggest planes, the A350, has 2.65 million parts!

Making the Wings

The wings are a really important part of the airplane. They have to be as strong and light as possible. The wings' frames consist of a rear **spar**, the main spar, and the ribs. These are made out of aluminum, one of the lightest metals.

A special kind of tape is used to cover the tops and bottoms of the wings. Before the tape is put on the wings, it's baked in a huge oven!

Building Blocks

After the wing tape is heated, it becomes stronger and lighter than steel!

Flaps move up and down on the wings to help the plane speed up or slow down. These flaps are controlled by the pilot in the cockpit.

The Body

The place where people sit in an airplane is called the fuselage (FYOO-suh-lazh). The fuselage is in the shape of a long, hollow tube. The pilots sit in the front of the fuselage in a closed area called the cockpit, where they control the plane.

The fuselage is made apart from the rest of the plane. The newest planes are made of special composite **materials**, or materials made of many different things. One example is carbon fiber, a very light material that's **woven** together to become very strong.

Building Blocks

Everything has a **center of gravity** to keep it balanced. A plane's center of gravity is in the fuselage. Wheels, which are part of the landing gear, are put under the fuselage so the plane doesn't tip over while on the ground.

cockpit

Lots of work goes into making sure the fuselage is safe
to walk around in for both the flight crew and the passengers.

Putting It All Together!

Now that the wings and the fuselage are finished, it's time to put the plane together. The nose, or front of the plane, is attached to the fuselage. Then the tail is added to the back of the plane.

The wings are attached to the sides. It takes some pretty big machines to get these huge pieces to fit together! The landing gear is then added. Finally, it's time to put the engines under the wings!

Building Blocks

The engines are always put on last, even after the cabin seats are put in! Once the engines are attached, the plane is tested to make sure it's ready for use. If a new plane is designed, it's taken out in every flight condition, just to make sure it's safe before making more of them!

Lots of screws and bolts are used to piece a plane together. Sometimes pieces are **welded** or **riveted** together, too!

Make Your Own Airplane!

Now that you know how an airplane's wings help it fly, let's learn how to make your own paper airplane.

What You Need:

- paper

How To:

1. fold a piece of paper in half vertically, then unfold with the crease facing down

2. fold the top two corners to the middle crease to make a point

3. flip the plane over and fold the two top corners in again to the center crease, making a more angled point

4. fold the paper in half against the vertical crease

5. fold the flaps down a few inches to make the wings

6. make sure your folds are even so it flies straight

7. try your paper airplane to see if it flies

Glossary

center of gravity: the place in an object that controls the balance for the whole object

design: to create the pattern or shape of something. Also, the pattern or shape of something.

engineer: a person trained in a profession that designs or builds machines

expert: someone with special skills or knowledge gained from training

material: the matter that something is made of

rivet: to connect two pieces of metal together using a metal bolt with a head at one end and a piece that is flattened into a head on the other end

runway: a paved strip of ground for the landing and takeoff of an airplane

simulation: the representation of the functioning of one system or process by means of another system

situation: the way in which events take place at a certain moment

spar: the steel skeleton of an airplane wing

vehicle: a machine used to move goods and people using an engine and wheels

weld: to heat two pieces of metal until they melt together and form one new piece

woven: having to do with a kind of material made by weaving, or the way of making something by overlapping thread, cloth, or other matter

For More Information

Books

Hammelef, Danielle S. *Building an Airplane*. North Mankato, MN: Capstone Press, 2014.

Nahum, Andrew. *Flight*. New York, NY: DK Publishing, 2011.

Websites

Fun Flight Facts for Kids
sciencekids.co.nz/sciencefacts/flight.html
Learn more about how an airplane works here!

NASA Kids Page: Airplanes
www.grc.nasa.gov/WWW/K-12/UEET/StudentSite/airplanes.html
Learn more about the parts of an airplane on this NASA site.

Index